Thank you to all of you safe distancing contributors, all around the world, who allowed me a place to be creative.

I, try to maintain a sense of civility in my life while staying in the house away from potential killing cooties.

I wake up, make my bed, do my ablutions, put on make up, get dressed up and proceed to the kitchen. I make coffee and breakfast and then ....eat it straight out of the pan over the kitchen sink.

Georgette Baker, March-May 2020

TABLE OF CONTENTS

You do it and add page numbers while you're at it

2020 came out all
looking like a warm
chocolate chip cookie.

Then one bite and
Bam. Oatmeal raisin.

LEMON ARTICHOKE PASTA

One 15 oz can of artichokes in water
2 lemons
2-3 tablespoons of Olive oil
1 clove freshly crushed garlic
1/8 tsp garlic salt
2 handfuls of fresh spinach, chopped
1 cup chicken broth
2 tablespoons chopped fresh rosemary
10 basil leaves chopped
1/4 cup grated Romano cheese
1/3 cup shredded Parmesan cheese
One 12 ounce box of pasta
A sprinkle of roasted pine nuts

Sauté garlic, chopped artichokes and spinach in olive oil
in sauté pan on low
Add chicken broth
Grate lemon rind into pan
Add juice from 2 lemons
Add rosemary and Romano cheese

Boil pasta (I used gluten free egg noodles)
Drain all but 2 tablespoons of water
Add 1/2 the sauté items into the pot
Mix in the pasta
Separate into serving bowls
Add remaining sauté on top of each dish
Sprinkle pine nuts and Parmesan cheese on top
Enjoy!

Submitted by Sharon Grandinetti

EASY BRISKET

1 whole brisket trimmed but with 1/2 fat (trimming optional, I don't)
Apples 4 Granny Smith
1 bottle Heinz chili sauce.
1 can Guinness draft
1 cup brown sugar
Spices mixed in a bowl parts of ground cumin paprika (cayenne pepper if you want a zing)
Rosemary salt black pepper.
(Go easy on the cayenne or separately do one side)

Oven at 275
1/2 aluminum disposable pan or large metal roasting pan
Pour 1/2 the Guinness over the brisket - drink the rest
rub spices on the brisket and place in the pan
Pour 1/2 the chili sauce on the top of the brisket
Slice applies and remove the core
Mix brown sugar apples in a large bowl and mix
Pour the other half 1/2 of the chili sauce in with the apples
Put a shot of bourbon or a shot of the Guinness in the empty chili sauce bottle, swish it and pour into the apple mix and pour and spread the apples mix over the brisket
Sprinkle another 1/4 cup of brown sugar over it.

Cook the brisket at 275 F. for 6 hours and baste it every hour or so.

You can cook it longer if desired and I like to start early and let it go 8-12 hours at 255 F.

Submitted by Jim Butler

BEST BREADED ITALIAN PORKCHOPS

3 eggs
3 Tablespoons milk
1 and 1/2 cups seasoned Italian bread crumbs
1/2 cup grated Parmesan cheese
2 Tablespoons dried parsley
2Tablespoons olive oil

1. Heat oven to 325 degrees
2. Get two small bowls out of your vast supply of bowls. They should be unbreakable.
3. In bowl 1, crack 3 eggs and beat violently
4. Add milk to the poor eggs.
5. In bowl 2, mix the bread crumbs, parm, and parsley.
6. Go to step 7
7. Put the oil into a cast iron skillet. No other type of skillet will do unless you just don't care. In that case any type of skillet will do.
8. Heat the oil on medium high heat until you are very afraid to touch it.
9. Dip one chop into the egg mixture. Then dip the same chop into the other mixture. Get it super even. Must be perfect.
10. Put the chop into the skillet.
11. Repeat the dipping process for the other 3 chops. Hurry! They all have to be in the skillet at the same time!
12. Wash your hands because by now they are covered in goop.
13. Cook 3 minutes on each side until each side looks browned.
14. Very carefully and with two hands, use all your muscles to lift the skillet into the oven.
15. Bake the skillet for 25 min or to an internal temp of 145.

Submitted by Susan J Butler Elder

CHEESY BAKED MACARONI & CHEESE

16 ounces uncooked elbow macaroni

1 stick of butter

1/3 cup of flour

3 teaspoons of yellow mustard

1 teaspoon seasoned or regular salt

5 cups of milk

36 (1.5 lb.) slices of deluxe American cheese or sharp cheddar cheese or any combination of your favorite cheeses.

Parsley and smoked paprika to garnish

Directions

Cook pasta according to package directions. Preheat oven to 375°F.

In large saucepan, over medium heat, melt butter; stir in flour, mustard and salt. Gradually stir in milk. Cook and stir until mixture thickens slightly and bubbles.

Reduce heat adding cheese slices gradually and continue to stir until melted. Reserve 10 slices of cheese to place on

Spray 13" x 9" baking dish with non-stick spray and spoon pasta top with the remaining slices of cheese and sprinkle parsley and smoked paprika to garnish. Bake 40 minutes or until golden brown and let stand 10 minutes. Makes 10-12 servings.

Donald Mohid

BREAKFAST HASH BROWNS

4 Idaho or russet large potato
1 Stick butter
1 Tbsp olive oil

Peel or wash the potatoes
Slice and cut to chunks of your preference. I slice them into 1/4 to 1/3 thick slices, ad then quarter them.

Put the potatoes into a large frying pan and fill with water. Cook on high heat until the water boils and simmer until potatoes are tender but not mushy.
Drain the water and add the butter and olive oil. Put heat back on high and turn every 5 minutes until brown.
Optionally you could add an onion or yuca to the mix.
Serve hot as part of your breakfast!

Submitted by Jim Butler

Anyone know what type of Bourbon to serve with hash browns?

BAGUETTES

400 gr Flour ("00" Flour is best, but you can use regular bread flour"
1 cup water
1 teaspoon salt
2 1/4 teaspoons yeast (if regular yeast activate the yeast with some of the water (warm) with a teaspoon of sugar)

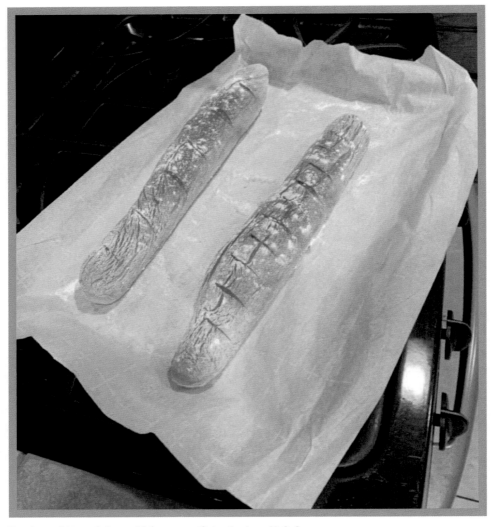

Submitted by Diane Steinheil Vargas

1. Mix all the ingredients
2. Let it sit in a bowl (covered with a humid towel) until it rises (1 hour)
3. Divide the dough in two and shape into to long baguettes. Lay it in a baguette pan or on a tray with parchment paper.
4. Place a pan with water in the lower rack of the oven
5. Pre heat the oven to 450 F and bake the baguettes until golden.

Delicious and so easy to make .... the house will smell wonderful and make you feel as if you were in Paris!

Artisan Bread

3 cups regular flour,

1 teaspoon salt

1/2 teaspoon yeast

1.5 cups of warm water.

(I sometimes add 1.5 cups shredded cheddar cheese).

Contributed by Annie Murnane

Using a wooden spoon, mix everything in a large bowl until combined. Cover with Saran wrap and leave at room temperature for 8-24 hours (I leave mine overnight).

90 minutes before you want it, turn dough onto a WELL-floured surface. It will be a gooey mess. Flour your hands and shape into a sorta-ball. With a sharp knife, cut an X in the top. Cover with a kitchen towel and let rest for around 30 minutes.

Meanwhile, get a tall-sided pot with a lid you can put in the oven. Put the pot in the oven and set the oven to 450 degrees, letting the pot heat in the oven. Once the oven reaches temperature, take the pot out, spray it with PAM. Pick up dough with well floured hands and plop it into the bottom of the pan. Put lid on it and bake for 30-35 minutes.

Remove lid and bake for another

15-20 minutes (until golden

brown). Let cool before

slicing.

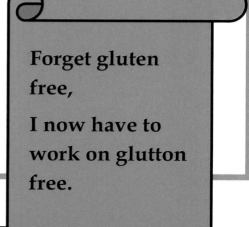

Forget gluten free,

I now have to work on glutton free.

CACHITOS DE JAMON

Little Venezuelan pastries filled with ham (jamon) shaped like a horn (Cachito). The recipe is for a large batch (1 kilo of flour) When I prepare them, I divide all the ingredients in half.

Ingredients:

1000 grams flour

100 grams milk

350 grams water

80 grams sugar

125 grams butter softened

1 package yeast

1 vanilla extract

10 grams salt

2 pounds ground or chopped ham I buy it at the honey baked ham already ground up

Directions:

1. Put some of the water (warm) in the mixing bowl with a bit of sugar add the yeast and let it sit for 10 minutes.

2. In the meanwhile, measure your ingredients and mix together flour, sugar and salt then add it to the yeast (after the yeast rises). Start the mixer going.

3. Add the softened butter and continue mixing

4. add the milk, water and vanilla, continue mixing...

5. Dough should be dry and separate from the bowl. Let it rest for an hour.

6. stretch the dough very thin with a roller (I do it in batches)

7. Cut in triangles (first cut a rectangle then cut the rectangle into two triangles

8. Put some ham on the triangle and roll it from the wide part towards the thin point

9. Place the rolls on a baking sheet (sprayed with PAM)

10. Brush over the rolls a mixture of egg yolk and a bit of water beaten

11. Bake at 350 F. until golden brown (30 to 40 min)

Submitted by Diane Steinheil Vargas

Tuscan Shrimp with spinach, mushrooms and sundried tomatoes

Ingredients:
1 pound large peeled shrimp
6 cloves garlic or more minced
2 tablespoons butter

1 tablespoon of sundried tomato oil
1/2 pound Pancetta cut small, if you don't have Pancetta then use bacon L
1 small white onion chopped small
1/2 cup sundried tomato packed in oil
1 cup heavy whipping cream

1 cup half and half

2 egg yolks
salt and pepper to taste
4 cups fresh baby spinach
1 cup Parmesan cheese freshly grated
1 teaspoon cornstarch mixed with a tbsp of water
2 teaspoons Italian seasoning
2 (8-ounce) packages white mushrooms **sliced and cooked in a hot pan to release and evaporate water**

Directions:

1. Melt 2 tablespoons of butter and a Tbsp of sundried tomato oil in a pan
2. Add minced garlic, cook for a minute or two
3. Add shrimp and cook lightly until both sides are pink, not cooked remove from pan and set aside
4. Add pancetta and cook one minute
5. Add onion and cook until transparent/slightly golden
6. Add sundried tomatoes cook 1 minute
7. Add cream and half and half and mix, heat until just before it boils

8. Add salt and pepper

9. Add spinach and cooked mushrooms and let it cook for a bit

10. Add Italian seasonings

11. Add shrimp

12 Add parmesan cheese

13. Mix the corn starch with a bit of water and add to the dish

14. Let it simmer, mixing slowly while sauce thickens a bit, for a few minutes until shrimp are cooked.

Serve with white rice or noodles, white wine and enjoy!!

Recipe & photo submitted by Diane Steinheil Vargas

BEEF FLANK STEAK MARINADE

4 parts L&P, 1 part bitters.
Add to that, 1/2 part apple cider, 1 part Soy Sauce, 2 parts olive oil, vinegar, and spices,
1 tsp cumin , 1/4 tsp thyme, 1/2 tsp turmeric,
1 -2 lb flank steak.

Put all ingredients into a large zip lock bag or bowl and mix together. marinade for at least 20 mins to 4 hours, (overnight if you're a planner)
Grill on a hot grill 6-8 mins per side.   Serve hot !

Submitted by Jim Butler

PLANNING WHERE TO GO OUT THIS WEEKEND

MUSHROOM SAUCE

1 large package of mushrooms

1 ½ cups of whipping cream

2 egg yolks

Dash of Worcestershire sauce

Salt, pepper, etc. to taste

Slice mushrooms and place in a pan

Cook at high heat (dry no butter), mushrooms will release water, keep cooking until they dry up

Add a tablespoon or two of butter

Apart mix 2 egg yolks with the whipping cream

Add to the mushrooms

Mushroom Sauce

Cook at high heat (dry no butter), mushrooms will release water, keep cooking until they dry up

Submitted by Diane Steinheil Vargas

RED PEPPERS á La OTRA

Cut two red bell peppers (morrón in Uruguay) in half

Prepare toppings by cutting up a few cherry tomatoes, chopping a few Spanish olives, snipping a small bunch of chives, cutting up a few fresh basil leaves. You can substitute for other items you might have on hand such as red onions, fresh cilantro, parsley, or capers. Set these aside for now.

Place the red peppers cut side down on the grill in direct heat. Watch that the flames do not scorch the peppers. After about 10 minutes flip so that the outside is now receiving direct heat. After about 5 minutes place a slab of provolone cheese (this is what is traditionally used in Uruguay), but any other cheese that will melt such as mozzarella can be used instead. Cook for about 5 minutes or until melted. Remove from flame and dress the melted cheese with the toppings you have prepared.

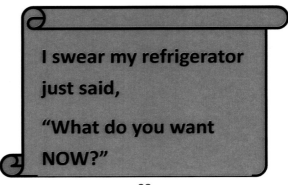

I swear my refrigerator just said,

"What do you want NOW?"

Submitted by Susan Pozo

CHINESE TEA LEAVES EGGS

1 dozen eggs

Cook in medium pot cover with cold water, bring to a boil, turn heat to medium for 5 minutes, then drain hot water out, fill pot with cold water to cool eggs down. Then remove eggs, put on paper towel n let dry.

Sauce:

1/3 c dark soy sauce

1/3 c light soy sauce

2 T fish sauce

1 t red pepper flake

4 clove garlic

2 T 5 spices powder

1/3 c any Chinese tea leaves

1/4 c bourbon or brandy

Put in 4 cups water and bring to a boil, then turn heat to med simmer for 1/2 hour, add 1 T honey, simmer 15 more minutes.

Use the inside of a table spoon to gently hit all side of each egg until the shells are crack but not detach.

Remove sauce from heat, soak all eggs in, make sure all eggs submerges, add water if needed. Let pot cool and fridge over night. Eggs can be eaten any time. Can use sauce as dip. Can reuse sauce for next batch or add sone sauce in noodle soup or rice.

Submitted by Sharon Tang

QUINOA SALAD

Add one cup of quinoa to 1 cup of boiling water.

Add salt to taste.

Let come to a boil and then let simmer until liquid has evaporated. The grains should now appear partly translucent.

Let quinoa cool while preparing about two cups of chopped vegetables to add.

In this case I used red and yellow peppers, cucumbers, cooked sugar peas, green onions and red cabbage. Other possibilities are tomatoes, zucchini, parsley, radishes, celery, corn. Small chunks of fresh mozzarella can also be added.

Prepare a vinaigrette totaling about 1/8th cup that is prepared by mixing together 3 parts olive oil to 1 part balsamic vinegar.

Mix the quinoa grains with the vegetable mix and stir in the vinaigrette. Salt to taste.

Can be eaten as is or when fully cooled. If allowed to sit overnight in the refrigerator, the vinaigrette will fully absorb, and the salad will be even more flavorful.

Submitted by Susan Pozo

CHOCOLATE **FUDGE BROWNIE CAKE** WITH CHOCOLATE GLAZE

The Cake

Chocolate cake mix; 15.25 ounce size box
Fudge brownie mix; 18.3 ounce size box
4 eggs
1 1/4 cup water
1 cup oil

For the homemade Glaze

1 cup heavy cream
12 ounces semi-sweet chocolate morsels

Add the ingredients for the cake in a large bowl and using either a stand mixer or hand mixer, mix for a few minutes. Pour batter into prepared bundt pan that's been sprayed with non-stick baking spray and bake for 50-55 minutes.

When done baking, remove cake and allow to cool in pan for up to five minutes. Run a knife along the edges of the cake pan to help release the cake and then carefully turn the cake out onto a cooling rack. Do not try to pour the glaze on top of the cake while it's warm.

Place heavy whipping cream in a microwave safe bowl and heat on high for two minutes or just until the heavy cream begins to boil.

Remove the bowl from the microwave and carefully add the chocolate morsels. The mixture may bubble up, this is okay! Let the mixture sit for 5 minutes and then begin to whisk until shiny and smooth, about 1 minute.

At first it may look like the glaze is not going to get smooth. But keep stirring and it will come together.

Pour over cooled cake and allow the glaze to drizzle down the sides of the cake.

Submitted by Annie Murnane Janulis Miles

PASSION FRUIT MOUSSE (Mousse de Parchita)

Smooth, silky, tangy, sexy wonderful desert!

Ingredients:
2 cups very cold whipping cream beaten
2 egg whites beaten
1 1/2 cups cold Passion Fruit (Maracuya) pulp
1 package gelatin dissolved in a bit of warm water
1/2 cup sugar
1 can sweetened condensed milk
Passion Fruit (Maracuya) seeds; mint etc for decoration

Directions:
1. Dissolve the gelatin in a bit of warm water or Passion Fruit liquid. Let it cool
2. Beat the egg whites until you can form little peaks with it
3. Beat the cream separately until it is nice and thick
4. Mix cream and egg whites together
5. Add condensed milk while mixing
6. Add the disolved gelatin to the passion fruit pulp (that should be liquid but cold)
7. Add the passion fruit to the creamy mixture.
8. Pour into individual bowls or one large glass bowl or a form
9. Decorate with passion fruit seeds or mint or both....
10. Refrigerate and be patient
11. About an hour later.... enjoy!

Recipe submitted by Diane Steinheil Vargas

BANANA CHOCOLATE CHIP
4H PURPLE RIBBON MUFFINS

Ingredients

2 1/2 C Flour

2 t. Baking powder

1 t. Baking soda

1 t. Salt

In separate bowl beat 1 C. Sugar

2/3 C. Butter or Shortening

Then fold in 4 eggs

Mix dry and wet together.

Beat ripe bananas and mix in. (We use all we have.)
Stir in the desired amount of chocolate chips.
Drop into muffin tins and bake at 400 for about 15-20
minutes.

I DON'T THINK ANYONE EXPECTED THAT WHEN WE CHANGED THE CLOCKS EARLIER THIS YEAR

WE'D GO FROM STANDARD TIME TO THE TWILIGHT ZONE

Submitted by Cindy Pfeiffer

PIZZA HOT DISH

This recipe has been in our family since the 1970s. Mom used to cook it all the time. It's quick to make, filling and tasty!

Ingredients:

1-2 lb of hamburger

Optional:

1/2 onion chopped

1/2-1 whole green pepper chopped

1 small can or 1 cup of fresh mushrooms chopped

12-15 pepperoni chopped

1 Jar of pizza sauce

2 cans of Crescent Rolls

1 bag of grated cheese, your choice

Preheat oven to 350

Sautee chosen ingredients and brown hamburger, drain. Add jar of pizza sauce and simmer on low.

Using a 13 x 8 baking dish, line the dish with the first can of crescent rolls, spread out using your fingers to push around the pan.

Add meat mixture and add your choice of grated cheese (mozzarella, cheddar, Mexican) 1/2 bag.

Place second can of crescent rolls on top of mixture, again spreading out.

Top with remaining cheese.

Bake at 350 for 25-30 minutes until crescent rolls are brown.

Serve alone or with your favorite vegetable or a salad.

Weekend
TRAVEL PLANS:
+ To the window
+ To the wall
+ Then I might skip down the hall

Submitted by Darrell Adams

BUTTERNUT SQUASH SOUP

½ cup unsalted butter

1 tablespoon olive oil

2 cups diced Vidalia or sweet onion

1 tablespoon minced garlic

2 tablespoons curry powder

2 teaspoons freshly grated ginger

1 tablespoon kosher salt

3 butternut squash (about 8 cups or 3 lbs.) peeled and cut into 1-inch chunks

8 cups

vegetable stock (or chicken stock)

2 cups coconut milk

NEW AIRPORT CODES

LVG Living Room	**MBR** Master Bedroom
DNG Dining Room	**OFC** Office
BTH Bathroom	**WNC** Wine Cellar
BKY Backyard	**HGR** Hangar
PAT Patio	**MNC** Man Cave

OPTIONAL GARNISH:

Sour Cream or Crème Fraiche

Chopped Chives

Submitted by Charlotte Creswell

VEGGIE NOODLE SOUP

Put a handful of any Chinese dry noodles in boiling   water, boil till noodles are almost soft, drain and run them through cold water, let sit and dry a bit in drainer.

Chop up 1/4 bunch of cleaned cilantro and 1 jalapeño.

Bring a can of chicken broth to boil with a tsp olive oil.

Add noodles and veggies in broth to boil for 1-2 minutes.

Serve in soup bowl, add a couple drops of sesame oil on top. Or a couple drops soy sauce if desired.

Submitted by Sharon Tang

HARD LIQUOR RAISINS

Fill any size jar with your choice of raisins..
Pour your choice of liquor over the raisins. (Gin. Vodka, whisky, rum, or brandy)

Let sit for a week at room temperature.

The longer it soaks, the better it tastes.
Can be used as snack while watching TV.
Add some into your glass of white wine.
Add them into your mixed salad.
People who don't like
alcohol replace the   liquor with Apple Cider Vinegar.

I have made both kinds.

I'm giving up drinking
until this is over.

Sorry, bad punctuation.
I'm giving up. Drinking
until this is over.

Submitted by Sharon Tang

VENEZUELAN PASTICHO

Ingredients:

Bechamel Sauce:

8 tablespoon of butter

4 tablespoons of flour

4 cups of milk, warm

1/2 teaspoon of salt

1/4 teaspoon of nutmeg

1/4 teaspoon of pepper

9 sheets of rolled flat lasagna pasta (I use Barilla - no boiling required)

8 cups of Bolognese Sauce (meat sauce)

2 cups of parmesan cheese, grated

Directions:

Prepare Bechamel sauce: In a medium pot, melt butter over medium heat. When butter has completely melted, add the flour and whisk until smooth, about 2 minutes. Gradually add the milk, whisking constantly to prevent any lumps from forming. Add salt, nutmeg and pepper and continue to simmer and whisk over medium heat until the sauce is thick, smooth and creamy, about 5 - 8 minutes. The sauce should be thick enough to coat the back of wooden spoon. Remove from heat and check for seasoning. Set aside.

Annie Murnane Janulis Miles

Preheat oven to 375º F. Line a large baking sheet with aluminum foil.

Butter a 13 x 9-inch baking dish. Spread 1/2 cup of the bechamel sauce into the bottom.

Assemble Pasticho: Arrange the 3 pasta sheets side by side, covering the bottom of the baking dish. Eve ly spread a layer of Bolognese sauce. Spread 1 1/2 cup of the bechamel sauce. Sprinkle 1/2 cup of parmesan cheese on top. Arrange another 3 pasta sheets, Bolognese sauce, bechamel sauce and parmesan Arrange the final layer of pasta sheets and top with remaining béchamel and Parmsan cheese.

Cover the lasagna dish with aluminum foil and place it on the baking sheet. Bake on the middle rack of the oven for 45 - 50 minutes, or until top is bubbling and the pasta is ender. Remove cover and continue to bake for about 15 minutes or until the cheese on top becomes golden.

Let stand for 8- 10 minutes before serving.

I'm having a quaran-
tine party this
weekend...
...........none of you
are invited.

SHRIMP SAUTEED IN OLIVE OIL

Cover bottom of pan with olive oil, add shrimp, salt and pepper to taste.

Turn shrimp when pink. When both side pink, remove from fire, serve up hot.

Submitted by Georgette Baker

I've done as much cooking while isolated as I did in 25 years of marriage. When this quarantine is over, the only thing I plan to make is reservations.

JALAPEÑO HOT WINGS

Ingredients

24 chicken wings (cut off the tips & discard, cut remaining wing at the joint)

Salt & Pepper

Season the wings with both salt & pepper

Preheat oven to 500 degrees and position 2 oven racks in the middle & upper third. Spread the wings out on 2 baking sheets in a single layer. Roast for about 40 minutes turning once, until wings are golden & crisp

(Or set the air fryer on 410 for about 20 minutes turning them once.)

Green Jalapeno Sauce

1/2 cup Green Jalapeno Hot Sauce (like Trader Joe's Green Dragon Sauce)

2 tablespoons coarsely chopped pickled jalapeno peppers

3/4 stick of unsalted butter

2 gloves garlic, minced

Puree the hot sauce and pickled jalapenos until smooth. In small saucepan cook the butter with garlic until fragrant, about 2 minutes. Add puree to saucepan and bring to a simmer. Transfer sauce to a large bowl. Using tongs transfer the wings to the bowl with the hot sauce and toss to coat.

Serve right away with the Blue Cheese dip.

Blue Cheese Dipping Sauce

¼ cup crumbled blue cheese

1 cup ranch style dressing

Mix or emulsify together and serve with the chicken wings

Submitted by Charlotte Creswell Brown

HALLACAS

Ingredients (Amounts depend on how many hallacas – calculate + /-)

-1 ½ lb Pork meat (cubed)

-1 ½ lb Beef meat (cubed)

-1 large Chicken (cut in pieces or two smaller chickens)

-3 Leek stalks (cut in small pieces)

-1 bunch Green onion (cut small)

-1 large Onion (cut small)

-1 Red and 1 green bell pepper (cleaned and cut small)

-4 Tomatoes (cut small)

-several garlic cloves

-1 bottle of Spanish Olives (pitted)

-1 bottle (small) capers

-1 bag of whole almonds (no skin)

-If you like some raisins soaked in rum

-2 carrots (for broth)

-2 celery pieces (for broth)

-1small onion cut small (for broth)

-1 bell pepper (for broth)

-Oil

-Onoto or (Anato) (If you can't find it then use yellow food color)

- Harina Pan

-Banana leaves

-thin rope

First – Chicken and chicken broth

1. Cut chicken into 6 pieces (2 breasts, two thighs, two legs)

2. Put in a deep pan with lots of water

3. Add carrots and celery cut in large pieces, bell pepper, onion, cut the hard green part of the leaves of the leeks and the green onions and add them in the pan with water (all this is to give flavor to the broth)

4. Add salt, pepper and any spices you like for flavor and cook

5. When chicken is cooked cut into small bite size pieces.

6. Separate broth from all the "stuff" added – Discard the "stuff" and keep broth in refrigerator.

Second - Onoto oil

1. In a pan add 2 cups of oil and heat

2. Add onoto pieces (red little balls) and let it cook for a bit until the onoto releases the color and flavor (don't taste it – it's HOT).

3. Separate the oil and discard the onoto.

(If you can't find Onoto then use Bijol or food coloring)

4. Add the pork and beef pieces and cook some more

Third - Sofrito and relleno

1. In a large pan add ½ cup of prepared onoto oil and heat up

2. Add the small cut pieces of: leeks, bell peppers, onion, green onion, and crushed garlic. Cook for a while until the ingredients appear cooked.

3. Add the cut tomato pieces and cook for a bit longer

5. Add the almonds, olives, capers. Cook and mix a bit. (If you were not able to get Onoto, now would be a good time to add food coloring or Bijol to give the "relleno" a good color.

6. Add the chicken pieces (don't cook the chicken to much or it will shred and disappear) and, if you like the raisins in the hallaca add them now.

7. If your sofrito is two liquid add some Wondra to thicken.

(By now you should be exhausted…. Drink a glass of wine and leave the rest for tomorrow or another day) So refrigerate or freeze your relleno and the broth.

Fourth - Prepare your masa

1. Depending on how many hallacas you are doing (based on the amount of relleno you have.) Warm up the broth a tad, make sure it tastes great (if not add flavor or salt etc)

2. To the broth add Harina Pan and mix constantly, add Onoto oil little by little (masa has to be nice and oily) – This is not arepa dough)

3. If you did not find Onoto then add Bijol or food coloring to broth before you add the Harina Pan.

4. Mix well and let it rest - check that the dough is soft but firm and of good color.

Ojo: If you find that you don't have enough broth for the masa, just add canned broth.

(By now your arms should be hurting from all that mixing of the dough, so it might be better if you find someone else to do the mixing…. hehehe)

Fifth – Prepare the Hallacas

1. Before you start, cut the strings with which you are going to tie your hallacas. Clean and cut your leaves to the size you want your hallacas to have (about 18 inches long, you should be able to wrap it like a little present).

2. With a soft cloth wipe some oil (onoto or other) on the leaf, spread dough (not to thick) put relleno, making sure there is at least one olive and a couple of almonds in each hallaca.

3. Fold the leaf, first one side, then the opposite side, then fold under the perpendicular sides…. I do a double wrap to make sure water stays out - Tie and VOILA!!!

The hallacas freeze great - I like to vacuum seal them for in each pack. (If not just put them in plastic bags and take as much air out of the bag before freezing.

SIXTH - Boil hallacas for about 10 minutes

1. In a large deep pan boil water, add hallacas and let them cook.

2. Serve on the plate with it's leaf under (looks cool)

3. Or if you are not eating them all prepare for freezing. ENJOY!!!

Submitted by Diane Steinheil Vargas

Honduran Quick Spaghetti

Ingredientes:

- 400 g bag of any kind of spaguetti but the best is either Fettuccine or Thick Spaggetti
- 1 Onion cut into julliane
- Jam, Bacon or Hotdogs cut into pieces (optional, the simple way is without meat but tastes better with. The amount is up to you.
- ½ Cup Heavy Cream (Mantequilla Crema/Nata Espesa)
- ½ Cup Ketchup, prefebly sweet, not tart
- ½ Cup Whole Milk (you can use skimmed but not the same)
- Hard White Latin Cheese, grated. You can also use parmesan or any other rated cheese.

Feeds around 6, depending on how hungry everyone is.

Preparation:

But water to boil and cool the pasta of your choice till it's to your taste. Prefrebly less since it then continues to soften when you throw it into the sauce.

Sauce:

Slightly fry the onion leaving it slightly crisp. If you use meat throw it in as well to fry a bit.

Throw in all the other ingredients and mix. The amounts are very changeable debending on your taste. I usually put more ketchup in. If the sauce is too thick, use more milk.

Once the pasta is cooked, drain and throw into the sauce.

Serve with your choice of grated cheese toping. Good with toasted garlic bread.

All set....Enjoy

Submitted by Miriam Boersner (as a pdf)

Oma's Chupe

This is a take on the Peruvian Chupe, a soup my mother (Oma) became famous for.

Ingredients for four:

- 4 Potatoes cut into cubes (I use the potato fries slicer to cut them into fries and then cube them). Put them in a bowl with enough water to cover them. This will avoid oxidation and it is the water you will use for the soup.
- 1 Red pepper cut into cubes (make sure to eliminate the white inner parts that can be bitter)
- 1 Onion cut into cubes
- 4 Slices of bacon cut into bits
- 1 Can Corn Grains
- 1 lb Small Peeled Shrimp Raw
- 1 Table Spoon Four
- ½ Cup Heavy Cream or Whipping Cream (not sweetened)
- 1 Envelope of dried Sea Food Cream Soup or equivalent. I use Crema Marinera Maggi or Knorr.
- Shrimp Broth Cubes for additional salting if needed. (optional)

Fry the bacon on medium heat. As soon as it lets go a bit of fat, throw in the onion and red pepper.

Once the bacon is slightly crisp and the onions look transparent, throw in the flour and stir to blend.

Immediately throw in the potatoes with all the water, you may have to add a little more water later if the soup gets too thick. Add the envelope of Sea Food Cream Soup. This adds taste and salt but usually the soup needs extra salt. You can salt with some more Sea Food Cream Soup or regular Salt, but do the extra salt last, salt to taste.

Let boil on medium/low stirring every once in a while so nothing sticks to the bottom of the pot. Cook for 15 to 20 minutes till the potatoes are cooked.

Add the corn and the Shrimp and let boil for another five minutes.

Add the Heavy Cream and let boil for another minute or two.

Serve with some good garlic bread or baguette. For the hot sauce lovers, a dash of Tabasco makes it even better.

ENJOY

Submitted by Miriam Boersner (as a pdf)

SPANAKOPITA-GREEK SPINACH PIE

Fresh spinach (large bag, wash and cut into small pieces)

2 bunches parsley leaves only, finely chopped

1 large yellow onion, finely chopped

extra virgin olive oil
4 eggs

10.5 oz quality feta cheese, crumbled

2 tsp dried dill weed

black pepper to taste

1 16 oz package Filo Dough

Chop onion and sauté in a deep pot, in olive oil, add spinach, sauté lightly, **not** cooking. **Drain all extra liquid.**

Remove from heat, add scrambled eggs, dill, feta, parsley. Let sit while filo is prepared

Lightly brushed with olive oil, the pan of your choice.

Lay 1 sheet of phyllo dough in baking pan and brush lightly with olive oil. Lay another sheet of phyllo dough on top, brush with olive oil, and repeat process with four more sheets of phyllo. The sheets will overlap the pan.

Spread spinach and cheese mixture into pan and fold over-hanging dough over filling.

Brush with oil, then layer remaining 4 sheets of phyllo dough, brushing each with oil.

Tuck overhanging dough into pan to seal filling.

Cut into squares (a wet knife works best) before baking.

Brush top filo with a little bit of water. Bake 325 for 1 hour.

Let it become golden brown on top.

 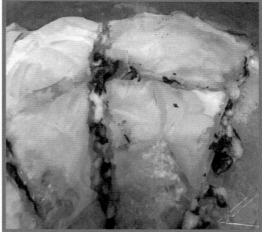

Submitted by Georgette Baker

KIMCHU GREEN SALSA NOODLES

Boil handful rice noodles and drain.
In a pot with 1.5 bowl boiling water
Add 1 cut up jalapeño, handful cut up cilantro
Add 1 tsp fish sauce, 1 tsp soy sauce, 1 tsp olive oil, 1/2 cup green salsa (I got a twin pk of red n green salsa from Costco, green one is very spicy)
Add noodles, turn off heat.
Dish everything in a large bowl.
Add 2-3 drops sesame oil.   Add Kimchi on top. Voila!!

Submitted by Sharon Tang

FAST FOOD

1 Pack of Udon noodle in boiling water for a few minute, then drain out water

In a second pot boil a bowlful of water with soup packet,

Add 1 cut up jalapeño and a handful of cut up garlic-chile (I used scissors).

Pour noodles in soup, add a few drops sesame oil and cut up 3 strips of pre-cooked bacon on top.

Submitted by Sharon Tang

MUSHROOM and GARLIC

Stir fry mixed mushrooms of your choice with garlic
Heat pot, add dash salt and olive oil,
Add 3 cloves garlic and brown them a bit
Add all mushrooms, stir them to prevent sticking,
Juice will come out, if too dry add little water,
Stir till look good, turn off heat.

Submitted by Sharon Tang

FRAGRANT FLOWER SOUP

Honey Suckles, fragrant rose petals, ginger, mandarin peels, and honey tea.

My honey suckles growing like crazy.

I picked the blooms and the almost bloom flower buds.

A few roses petals (Angel face, memorial day, rock n roll, double delight, and stainless steel are very fragrant that in my garden)

Skinned Ginger roots cut in thin strips,

Cleaned mandarin peels cut into small pieces,

All in mug and pour in boiling water,

Let   sit

Submitted by Sharon Tang

The most challenging experience (s) of this stay in place experience is not enjoying my walks as much as I used to. Too many people on my favorite routes. And I miss enjoying a nice meal in a restaurant with a friend. And miss hugs. Charlotte

My days went from a busy cycle of family and exercise to long, lonely walks on the trail by myself or with my husband and three dogs. I learned to keep worry from my mind by focusing on the natural beauty, changing season, interesting flowers, and birds. Cindy

The most challenging experience (s) of this stay in place mandate is overeating and not burning it off playing racquetball. Giving less hugs and being constantly conscious to stay free of germs I could accidentally pass on to my newborn granddaughter. I must remind myself daily that I create the fear I feel and work to continuously dissipate it.

Not being able to go to live events like baseball games or concerts. Darrell Adams

Have to miss all the wild flowers in bloom. Sharon Tang

Not being able to fly in order to help my son and daughter-in-law with their 2 month old during a difficult time; observing the dismay of employees who were at risk of losing their jobs. Both were profoundly disappointing and sad experiences. Susan Pozo

To helplessly see so much death and sorrow happen in such a short time. Diane Steinheil Vargas

Learning how to effectively work from home and remaining productive Jim Butler

Keeping my sanity. I miss human interaction, hugs and conversation. Donald Mohid

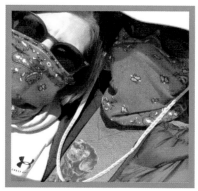

Pasta flambee?

Blackened Pasta?

Pasta al diablo?

Firehouse Special?

Hot Angel Pasta?

Posted by Good Living Guide

5/12/2020 Morning mishap, how can I rescue them short of eating them?

Ann Nguyen I will use the for my Egg Drop Soup! Ha

Sharon Tang Scoop them up with junk mail hard cards, put in a bowl, mix a bit flour, make a mask for ur skin.

Evangelia Deslis beat them with olive oil, great mask for your hair. Keep the hair covered with a dump towel for 20 minutes.

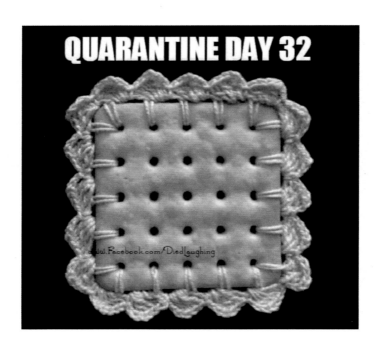

QUARANTINE DAY 32

Just about when we thought things were going to change, they did....

Made in the USA
San Bernardino, CA
09 June 2020

72648911R00042